From Blue to Digital Gold

From Blue to Digital Gold
The New American Dream

Paul Alex Espinoza

All Rights Reserved. No portion of this book may be reproduced, stored in a retrieval system, or transmitted in any form or by any means – electronic, mechanical, photocopy, recording, scanning, or other – except for brief quotations in critical reviews or articles without the prior permission of the author.

Published by Game Changer Publishing

Paperback ISBN: 978-1-962656-05-4
Hardcover ISBN: 978-1-962656-06-1
Digital: ISBN: 978-1-962656-07-8

www.GameChangerPublishing.com

DEDICATION

To my mother, whose relentless work ethic and indomitable spirit became the guiding light for my own mindset. Your strength is the blueprint of my story.

Thank you.

To all first responders, whose dedication paints the thin blue line bolder and brighter. From a detective who knows the heart behind the badge, I salute the excellence and integrity of good police work.

Always.

To every aspiring entrepreneur and dedicated 9-5er: May the pages ahead fuel your fire and illuminate your path, turning dreams into tangible realities and daily grind into lasting legacy.

Here's to the bold journey of building your own empire.

Read This First

I want to provide you with some additional value to help you on your entrepreneurship journey. Go to the website below to claim one of your FREE gifts from me.

www.officialpaulalex.com/Thankyou2023

From Blue to Digital Gold

The New American Dream

Paul Alex Espinoza

www.GameChangerPublishing.com

Foreword

When we hear about detectives, our minds often conjure up images of gritty crime scenes, suspenseful interrogations, and that relentless pursuit of truth.

Rarely do we associate them with the world of entrepreneurship.

That was until I read into the story of a former detective who navigated the maze of business ventures, shattering the mold of conventional career paths and inspiring countless others, including myself, to do the same.

This real story of a detective-turned-serial-entrepreneur serves as an emblem of transformation.

Transitioning from the world of law enforcement into the realms of passive income ventures and digital marketing, this detective demonstrated that the skills acquired in one field could be ingeniously adapted to another.

Observant eyes trained to spot discrepancies in a suspect's story were now identifying trending business ventures.

The strategic mindset that once solved intricate cases was now designing multifaceted business campaigns.

For me, a police sergeant content in my role and responsibilities, this tale was a revelation.

It spoke of possibilities beyond the uniform, of harnessing innate skills and applying them to the vast, dynamic world of entrepreneurship.

It was the push I needed. If Paul could transition and thrive, couldn't I, with my wealth of experiences and knowledge, do the same?

Reading about Paul's journey from the police department to building true wealth from undercover surveillances to bootstrapped startups, I realized that being an entrepreneur wasn't just about business acumen.

It was about adaptability, resilience, and a perpetual hunger for learning. It was about seeing opportunities in challenges and daring to step outside one's comfort zone.

To Paul, whose story is etched in these pages, thank you for lighting the path for the rest of us.

To you, the reader, may this narrative ignite in you the same drive and vision it did in me.

Here's to our shared journey of evolution, transformation, and boundless potential.

— Gedam Tekle, Former Police Sergeant turned Full-Time Entrepreneur.

Table of Contents

Introduction 1

Chapter 1 – Where It All Started Law Enforcement and Becoming a Leader . 5

Chapter 2 – Developing a Millionaire's Mindset 33

Chapter 3 – The ATM Side Hustle 43

Chapter 4 – The Credit Card Machine Business 61

Chapter 5 – Self Education and Digital Marketing 67

Chapter 6 – The Traits of Leadership and Business 85

Conclusion – What's Next? 91

Introduction

Who Is This Book For?

If you're holding this book right now, there's a possibility that you're sitting in a cubicle or an office space, staring at a computer screen and pondering whether there's more to life than your current situation.

I'm referring to your 9 to 5 job...

The good news? This book is for you. If you've ever dreamed of breaking the shackles of the nine-to-five grind, taking control of your financial destiny, exploring the world of entrepreneurship, building something you're passionate about, creating jobs, or making a positive impact in your community, then keep reading.

This book caters to the inspiring entrepreneur, the dreamer, the late bloomer, and those in need of extra motivation to overcome roadblocks in their journey. If you've dreamt of owning a business but don't know where to start, this book will be your roadmap.

For those who've daydreamed about big ideas while enduring their day job—just like my time as a cop in one of the most dangerous cities in the United States—this is for you. For the side hustler who's taken that brave first step into entrepreneurship, whether it's an ATM business, digital marketing, or selling flowers on the weekend, this book offers guidance on leveling up to full-time entrepreneurship.

Believe it or not, age is just a number. If you think you might be too old to start anew, you'll find examples here of successful entrepreneurs who began later in life, proving it's never too late.

What Can You Expect From This Book?

Knowledge: Equip yourself with insights on starting and running a business. Drawing from various business models I've initiated while working my 9-5 job, this book will bolster your confidence.

Skills: Dive deep into essential skills like time management, networking, negotiation, and leadership as I detail my journey from side hustles to multimillion-dollar enterprises.

Mindset: Arguably the most critical transformation you'll undergo. Adopting a resilient mindset is vital. I'll guide you through the metamorphosis I underwent.

A Roadmap: A step-by-step guide adaptable to your unique situation, serving as a blueprint through the highs and lows of your entrepreneurial odyssey.

Think of this book as a treasure trove of wisdom, tools, and life experiences designed to make your entrepreneurial dreams a reality.

Let's embark on this thrilling journey. The road ahead might be tough, but it promises adventure and fulfillment beyond your wildest dreams.

Who Is Paul Alex, and Why Heed His Advice?

In 2017, as a detective in law enforcement, I delved into a side hustle—setting up ATM businesses, all while working in one of the most perilous cities in the U.S. By 2020, I ventured into digital marketing, aiding thousands in establishing their ATM enterprises across the nation.

Since then, I've guided over 2,600 entrepreneurs in launching their own ATM businesses. In January 2021, I founded a digital marketing venture focused on the ATM sector. This business, ATMtogether.com, generated over $20 million in revenue. The proceeds were channeled into expanding my brand and enhancing my social media presence, which assists thousands of entrepreneurs daily.

I've roamed the world, wielding the freedom to work anywhere and help aspiring entrepreneurs succeed through simple businesses. Additionally, my journey as a professional speaker generated over $5 million from stage appearances, podcasts, and webinars.

How Did I Break Free From the 9 to 5 Routine?

At my core, I'm a nine-to-fiver with a dream—a dream of being able to provide for family and financial freedom. I didn't have a blueprint due to my background and upbringing. The hard lessons were my teachers.

Having been a serial entrepreneur for over a decade, juggling corporate America, law enforcement, and finally becoming a full-time entrepreneur in my early 30s, I've discerned the pivotal role of mindset. It was this mindset that liberated me from my nine-to-five grind. As you delve into this book, I hope my journey to entrepreneurship inspires your own transformation.

CHAPTER 1

Where It All Started
Law Enforcement and Becoming a Leader

In 2014, I was 26 years old and a Territory Sales manager in the San Francisco Bay Area for a large, multi-billion dollar chemical cleaning company.

At that time in my life, I had about six years of sales experience in corporate America. I was making six figures annually and also organizing nightlife events as a side hustle. I had a nice condo. I thought I had everything figured out, but I wasn't fulfilled.

I was dating a girl who I had been in a relationship with for seven years. I had told her I was not happy. She asked me, "What do you want to do in life?"

Growing up, my parents always told me, "Do the right thing. Go for the American dream." And what is the American dream? The American dream to my parents, who were immigrants from Peru and Mexico, and who had worked hard their entire life, was to get a good paying job, buy a house, find the love of your life, get married, have kids, and retire.

That's what life is all about. Well, I was almost there, except I wasn't married at the time.

I was in a very serious relationship. I had a great job. I went through the ranks, starting as a dishwashing repair guy in corporate America to becoming a salesman, a sales executive, and then finally a Territory Sales manager for the company. I was one of the youngest sales guys. I thought I had it all figured out.

Then, I had a conversation with my ex's cousin, who at that time was the sergeant of police in the San Francisco Bay Area. During that conversation, I told him, "Hey, man, I'm looking for a change. I need something different. This job? I've been in sales my entire life since almost the age of 21, and I'm not even supposed to be here." I didn't know what direction I was going to go in life. I didn't have any serious mentors knowledgeable about building a business or being career-driven. All I had was the advice of my parents, which was to work hard.

He told me, "Dude, you know how to talk to people. You're actually very motivating. You're ambitious, optimistic, and charismatic. You should become a cop."

And at that moment, I still remember that conversation while we were at Five Guys, a burger place in the Bay Area. I thought, *Me? A cop?* I never thought as a kid I would be a cop. I used to be very scared of them.

So, I did my due diligence and really looked into it. The process of becoming a cop is extensive. It involves several steps, including oral board interviews, physical agility tests, lie detector tests, and more. I applied to a dozen police agencies in the San Francisco Bay Area. I was focused on working in one of the most dangerous cities in the United States, which was Oakland, California.

After a long and challenging process, I finally got accepted into the police academy. Once I got in, I treated every day like it could be my last. The training was rigorous and intense. By the end of the six-month program, about 50% of the candidates dropped out. We had hundreds of hours dedicated to various forms of training.

The day I graduated from the police academy was one of the proudest moments in my life. I remember starting the very next day. When I asked my recruiting instructor which shift I was working, he told me it was the night shift. My first night was a mixture of fear and excitement. Over time, I became more comfortable in my role.

My first month as a police officer was filled with intense situations, particularly domestic violence incidents. My FTO even predicted that I would become a detective based on my performance. After three months of field training, I was assigned to East Oakland, one of the city's most challenging areas. But I was told that I could handle it, and I was ready for the challenge.

"Pressure creates diamonds," and after working in law enforcement, I am proof that the saying is very true.

"Paul, you're going to be very successful in law enforcement." These are the last words that my field training officer told me before he shook my hand and said, "Congratulations, you have passed field training."

After that, I experienced a full year of different incidents that molded me into a leader. I loved talking to the people in the neighborhoods that were part of my

patrol beat. I still had the entrepreneurial spirit inside of me, and I would talk to the local business owners about marketing, sales, and how they started before launching their own businesses.

I remember walking around the neighborhoods to show police presence and random people would approach me, saying, "Officer Espinoza, thank you." It was a very rewarding career at that time, my first year as a police officer.

Being proactive in law enforcement means that you are actively looking for illegal activity based on intelligence-based policing. I knew the neighborhoods I patrolled intimately. Specific areas were known for high narcotic activity and housed gang members known to carry weapons. That's where I concentrated my efforts, intending to make a tangible impact.

Every morning at 6 AM, after roll call, I would set out in a black and white, fully marked Ford Crown Vic. I would research the recent crime trends for the week, aiming to make a difference by identifying the most wanted criminals listed by our Criminal Investigation Division (CID).

Daily, our department would circulate the top 10 list of most wanted criminals. Studying this list and conducting my own investigations was part of my routine. Growing up, I never had an affinity for reading, but in police work, 90% of the job is about reading and writing reports. Each night and before every shift, my research would focus on this wanted list.

Within eight months of concluding my field training, my dedication bore fruit. I was awarded a captain's commendation for arresting over 10 of the most dangerous criminals from that list. This achievement began to build my reputation within the department.

One day, a police captain approached me. "Paul, you do good police work. I'm going to recommend you for the CRT." At that time, CRT stood for Crime Reduction Team. It was rare for new officers to be considered for these specialized units. I felt a mix of intimidation and excitement. While it meant leaving behind my status as one of the best in my current unit, the opportunity to grow was irresistible.

However, whispers spread. Some officers questioned my rapid ascent, remarking, "Who does he think he is? He's still a rookie." But others saw the quality of my work and my passion, and they supported me.

Joining the crime reduction unit was a transformative experience. While I started my police career as an introvert, this new role forced me out of my shell. My sergeant, a figure of authority and respect in the department, demanded nothing short of excellence. He instilled in us the importance of detail in our reports, a skill that would later prove invaluable in my detective role.

The sergeant's discipline and paramilitary leadership style were a challenge to adapt to. His critique was direct; if a report wasn't up to standard, he'd say so. And he constantly pushed me to assert myself more in the field.

Over time, this rigorous environment shaped me. I grew from an introvert to an extrovert, gaining confidence with each passing month.

By the end of my first year, the achievements I had amassed made me walk taller and prouder. I had not only learned how to draft search warrants but had also presented them to judges. I had spearheaded numerous gang-affiliated investigations.

One of the most memorable experiences during that period involved an investigation of a robbery crew. Consisting of two young men and a woman, they were behind a series of robberies and carjackings. Our mission was to unravel their MO (Method of Operation).

Then, on a cold, rainy day in East Oakland, an undercover officer spotted the crew we had been tracking. My sergeant's voice crackled over the radio, "Hey, guys, we've located the robbery crew. The captain wants us to make the arrest."

I remember going to a parking lot where we all met, and our Sergeant told us this: "All right, guys, in the next two minutes, we are going to face one of the most dangerous robbery crews we have seen in the past year. They have committed several robberies with assault rifles and have carjacked a Mercedes vehicle that is worth over $100,000. We've spotted the vehicle, and they're currently at a specific location in East Oakland."

My heart was racing. My heart was racing because I didn't really have any time to process what we were about to do.

My Sergeant said, "Guys, get ready. Paul, you and your partner, you're going to go ahead and do a vehicle stop on these criminals. And we're going to take them to jail."

So, we all got in our patrol vehicles, and as the undercover unit saw the three suspects get into the stolen vehicle, they started driving. Well, as we went behind them and I turned on my police vehicle lights, all of a sudden, the suspect vehicle started accelerating faster and running through stop signs and red lights.

And at that time, I still remember my heart racing because it was the very first time I got into a vehicle chase.

I remember during the vehicle chase, the suspects were throwing handguns while going through these neighborhood streets. There were innocent civilians just watering their lawns, watching with mouths agape and eyes wide as the vehicle with the criminals drove past them, going 50-60 miles per hour.

I then remember the three criminals crashing into a light pole. At this time, it was getting dark, and I remember the suspects jumping out of the car and running in different directions.

Now, at this time, the suspects had crashed the vehicle. We put the information about the vehicle crash and the direction the suspects headed towards on the radio, so we were able to get more officers on their way to our scene to help.

"Guys, we have three suspects potentially armed. They committed multiple robberies and carjackings. We need every single unit to block off a perimeter so we can search the yards of where they possibly went to."

I remember that day like it was yesterday. I remember it was getting dark. We called the California Highway Patrol to help us with their helicopters because they had special lights to light up the entire street block where the suspects could have gone.

My sergeant told my team, "You guys are the best of the best for a reason. Grab your flashlights. You guys are going to be hand-checking about five to six homes for these criminals that are possibly in the backyard of one of these residences. Go in with partners and be very careful."

I remember we checked multiple backyards, and one by one, we found each of these criminals and arrested them.

I was supposed to be home by 9 PM that day. I remember while we were still at the police station at 1 AM finishing the reports after we took those three criminals to jail, my ex-girlfriend texted me, "Are you still working?"

I texted her back, "Yes, I'm probably going to be here till about 3 AM writing my report. I'm sorry."

I remember being so tired that my eyes were bloodshot red. Even drinking coffee wouldn't keep me up. That's when I started drinking energy drinks, which caused me to have heart issues later in my life. I would take 20-minute power naps every few hours between shifts or during 18-hour work days.

I remember driving back home when the sun was coming up the next day. It became a weekly occurrence that we would have 1-2 days just like that. We were considered a proactive team, and that's what we signed up for. I never worked so much in my life, but I was happy. I felt fulfilled doing great police work!

For some reason, ever since I became a cop, I always told myself, "I want to be a narcotics detective." So, one day, I had just arrested a known drug dealer who was a felon in possession of a firearm. I was giving the suspect a traffic ticket, and during the traffic stop, I found out he was on parole with a search clause. While I was searching him, I found a loaded handgun in his front waistband. So, while I was at the jail dropping off the suspect, I saw a blacked-out Chevy Tahoe with tinted windows. I wondered, "Who the heck is this? FBI? CIA? DEA?"

It was a friend of mine, someone I hadn't seen for a year. "Hey, man, where have you been?" I asked.

My friend replied, "Oh, dude, I got picked to be a narcotics detective for this specialized narcotics task force. We investigate high-level narcotic traffickers that move millions of dollars of narcotics monthly."

That moment stuck with me. I was just in awe… How was it possible that my friend got into that specialized task force?

After talking to my friend a few more times, I learned that he was working under the County Sheriff's department in charge of that task force. They would hand-pick one detective from 13 different agencies across the county. This task force is an undercover unit investigating some of the biggest narcotic traffickers in Northern California.

But before I get into that, I want to offer some advice. If you're considering getting into law enforcement, especially in 2023-2024, heed my words: Don't join for the paycheck. Yes, you can make good money depending on where you work as a police officer in the U.S. As a first responder, most police agencies offer unlimited overtime. But law enforcement made me a leader, and I was able to apply those skills in entrepreneurship. It molded me into the person I am today. Without my law enforcement experience, I wouldn't have built two different multimillion-dollar businesses.

So, if you're reading this for inspiration because of my background in law enforcement, business, or sales, and you're considering a career in law enforcement or advising someone else, ensure the motivation is genuine. If there's a true desire to protect and serve, then sign up. It's a profoundly rewarding job. In my opinion, the world doesn't always see the dedication and hard work of countless officers.

In 2017, I was reading my work emails when I came across this message: "Opening for Detective position in Countywide Narcotics Task Force."

My eyes opened wide, and I remember being so happy, saying, "This is my opportunity to move into the next goal of mine in law enforcement."

I applied alongside several other officers from different specialized units in my department, the best of the best.

I remember that after a few months and following the interview with the Lieutenant and the sergeants of the narcotics task force, I received an email.

I recall it was about 6 AM on a Saturday morning. I checked my email application on my phone and saw a message from the Lieutenant of this unit. It read, "Hey, Paul, congratulations. You placed number one to become a Detective for the Narcotics Task Force."

I couldn't believe it. I was so excited. Something I had really wanted was finally happening. They gave me a few weeks to prepare and told me, "You're going to start with us at the end of the month. Be at this location at 6 AM in the morning because we have our first operation."

To be honest, the news spread like wildfire across the police station. I had officers who knew me showing me a great amount of support, while others I didn't speak to or know well said, "You're not ready," "Who do you think you are?" and "You think you're better than us?" People were talking behind my back. I remember hearing other officers talking down about me during line-up.

"That task force unit, he's going to be working with other detectives from 11 different police agencies in the county that have anywhere between 10 to 20 years of experience. And this kid, with two years of experience, thinks he has what it takes to be a detective in the narcotics task force? He must be out of his mind."

I didn't care. I didn't care about what they had to say because I knew I could do it. I had a winning mindset, and that's what separated me from the majority of everyone else who started around the same time as me in law enforcement. My mindset was bulletproof. Every time somebody told me that I couldn't do something, I'd prove them wrong. Anytime somebody would throw shade, hate, or negativity my way, I would go ahead and prove them wrong. I put my head down and got to work. I always let my results speak.

I showed up on the first day at the Narcotics Task Force building in Oakland, CA. I entered the building, and I remember there had to be

50+ police officers, along with federal agents from the FBI, the DEA, Homeland Security, U.S. Marshals, and various other agencies. I was the new kid on the block. I recall a female detective from the unit approaching me because the task force was primarily male-dominated. She said, "Hey, nice to meet you. You're the new guy. Here's your uniform. Get into the meeting room with everyone else, and the Lieutenant is going to brief us on our first operation."

I remember putting on that uniform, being in awe, and also telling myself, "What am I doing?" I sneaked through the back of the meeting behind everybody because I just didn't want to sit in the front. I listened in to the briefing of the Lieutenant, and I still remember the briefing.

The lieutenant was standing in front of the entire room, wearing his leather brown cowboy boots that he would wear at every single raid or operation. He always said they were his lucky boots, which is why his Task Force was the best in the state.

As the briefing started, the lieutenant spoke with extreme confidence. "All right, guys, we are doing a major operation today that we've been working on for months. We just busted a major narcotics trafficker with a million dollars in a suitcase. Now, we've traced the money back to 21 houses that are illegally growing marijuana. Some of these houses may be armed with people carrying assault rifles, handguns, etc. We don't know what we're going to deal with in the house, but we're going in there with everything we have and the resources to handle anything, guys. And where's the new guy?"

I remember everybody looking around, and I'm in the back of this 50-person meeting briefing, and I raised my hand, "I'm here, sir."

"New guy, you work in Oakland, right?" stated the lieutenant.

"Yes, sir!" I replied.

"You're driving the Batmobile," stated the lieutenant.

I said, "Excuse me, sir?"

"You're driving the entire task force in the SWAT tank because you have the best knowledge of the city you worked in," stated the lieutenant.

As I got into that Batmobile, which is what the Task Force called their armored tank, I've driven many cars in my life, but I've never driven a 15,000-pound vehicle in my life. That thing was massive. I remember 12 detectives suited and booted in SWAT tactical gear with their AR-15s, multiple rifle-rated vests, tactical headsets, helmets, and goggles, a few of them praying, and a few of them just talking normally. Then, one of them, in particular, approached me.

"Hey, so you're the new guy, huh?" stated the Detective.

"I am, sir," I advised.

"Don't call me, sir. I'm actually from one of the other local police departments, and I just wanted to introduce myself to you. I'm actually going to be training you for the first three months while you're in this unit because I want to make sure you don't get killed," the Detective stated.

At that time, that one detective, for the purposes of this book, we will call him Nick. Nick, later on in this chapter, you guys will see that he was actually my mentor for the task force. Nick nurtured me to be one of the best detectives on the task force and also for my police agency.

As the operation started, I drove the SWAT tank with the 12 detectives inside. As we approached one of the target houses, which was supposed to be an illegal marijuana grow house at that time, I remember the Lieutenant saying, "All right, guys, as soon as we hit the corner, Paul, you're going to drive the SWAT tank inside the living room of that house."

I must have driven the SWAT tank at five miles per hour down the street, with the Lieutenant yelling at me, "Faster, Faster, Faster!" As I was shaking, gripping the steering wheel, all I remember was the front of the SWAT tank was in the middle of the living room. The 12 detectives, including the Lieutenant, were throwing flashbangs, and I heard, "This is a police raid. Everybody, put your hands up." And in the back of my mind, I was just like, "My family is not going to believe me." "No one's going to believe me back in my agency that this was my first day."

Nick showed me how to recruit and also have working relationships with informants. In this specific unit, it was a plainclothes, undercover unit where we weren't in police uniforms. We would use regular vehicles to go ahead and work undercover operations at all times. The way we were able to infiltrate these large, large narcotic organizations was with informants' reliable information.

My first year, I worked roughly over 100 operations. That was about 8-10 operations monthly. As I was involved in every operation, my skill level grew with time.

My confidence level went from being an introvert to an outgoing extrovert that takes the lead and was a case agent for the remaining time that I was at that task force.

If it wasn't for that specific unit, if it wasn't for me having a mentor, I wouldn't have learned the skills that I have today to execute and lead a couple multimillion-dollar businesses, which I'm going to talk about later in the book.

But what you can take away from this as you read more into this chapter is that every life experience that you go through in life is a learning experience. Take what you can and implement it for the future. It's going to help you.

My second year on the task force, I was a different person. I was extremely confident and outgoing, and I had even more ambition to be the number #1 Detective in my unit.

During my time at TaskForce, I was managing approximately 32 informants. I represented my police agency well, and my agency awarded me for my efforts.

To be honest, I thought I was going to get fired.

During the meeting with the command staff of my police agency, I had my lieutenant say, "Paul, you do good police work."

So this is what we're going to do for you. We know that you work a ton of hours. At that time, I was working anywhere between 60 to 100 hours a week. But you know what? I wasn't complaining because I was doing my dream job. I was fulfilled, and I was having fun doing it. It was the greatest job in the world. It was something that you would see in movies. It was things that kids who always wanted to be cops in law enforcement or superheroes dreamed of.

And I was there actually doing it.

The Lieutenant says, "Paul, we're going to give you a partner."

We're going to let you handpick anyone you want from the police department.

I approached two of my friends, who were officers in my police department.

My first friend that I approached said, "I'm not ready. I don't have the experience you have."

I asked my second friend if he would like to be my partner, and he said, "When do I start?"

My new partner at the Taskforce, whom we'll call Hugh for the remainder of this chapter.

Hugh and I did every operation together. It worked out extremely well because I ran it like a business. I would have a specific role in the operations, like finding information from the informants and creating the game plan like a visionary.

I was the brains of the operations.

Hugh would run the infrastructure of the operations just like a Chief Operating Officer.

We were very proactive detectives, and we actually were able to do anywhere between 5 to 10 operations a month combined together on top of every other operation the other Detectives brought to the table.

At the end of my second year, I was awarded Top Detective of the Year out of 12 Agencies. It was the very first time my agency had won that award out of the 12 agencies that were involved in that task force.

I was proud.

My family was proud.

My girlfriend was proud.

I was on top of the world.

Just like everything in life, what goes up must come down.

A few weeks after winning that award, I was working on a huge case investigating a large cocaine trafficker out of Los Angeles.

We had already raided his house and caught him with almost a million dollars in cash from narcotic trafficking and a ton of drug paraphernalia.

However, the suspect was released from jail within 48 hours.

Somebody had bailed him out on a six-figure bail. Crazy…

I still had information on this large narcotic trafficker that he was still selling large amounts of cocaine after he went to jail.

I was able to gather enough information to execute another operation to catch the suspect with large amounts of cocaine.

I remember during the briefing of this specific operation that I had, I told everybody, "Guys, I just got information that this guy is at a hotel nearby and he's supposed to be in possession of multiple kilos of cocaine and hundreds of thousands of dollars in proceeds of narcotic trafficking."

So, we set up an undercover operation.

During the operation, we observed several narcotic traffickers going in and out of that specific hotel room.

We stopped these narcotic traffickers.

We caught one with tens of thousands of dollars in money in a backpack.

Another narcotic trafficker we caught with 10 pounds of heroin.

My team had enough evidence to write a search warrant for this hotel room where the suspect and narcotics were being stored.

At that time, my entire team wasn't present during this operation.

There were only seven of us, seven detectives, and it was my operation.

I remember telling my sergeant and my lieutenant, "Guys, this guy is inside the hotel room, and he's going to have kilos of cocaine based on the reliable information that I have received. Based on the evidence and information I gathered during the undercover operation, a search warrant was approved by a judge.

I remember everybody's face that day.

My team was eager to arrest this suspect because he was continuing to flood the community with narcotics, which leads to more property, violent, and general crimes rising in our communities.

I remember a specific detective with whom I actually grew a great working relationship. He was the best tactical detective that we had.

He was part of the SWAT team for his police agency, and he was very diverse with firearms tactics.

He was the first Detective to breach the hotel room door where the narcotic trafficker was.

I was one of the first Detectives going inside that room.

As we breached the door, the suspect was lying on the bed.

I remember as our team went into the room, the bed was on the right-hand side.

The suspect got up with his mouth open and his eyes wide open, and I could see a white powdery substance on his chest.

It appeared as if he was sniffing on a narcotic substance.

As the suspect got up while we were going into the hotel room, this powdery substance went into the air.

As it went into the air, the majority of the narcotic substance actually landed on the first detective that went through the room first, my partner.

And for the purposes of this chapter, we are going to call him Jay.

Jay, within seconds, stated, "Guys, I don't feel that well."

At that time, everything happened within seconds.

My team had arrested the suspect.

My team recovered the cocaine as evidence in the hotel room.

And Jay comes up to me, and he's sweating profusely.

His lips were blue…

His fingertips were blue…

And immediately, I said, "Take off your gear."

At the time, the SWAT gear that we would wear when we would go and raid houses, rooms, whatever it was, weighed anywhere between 60 to 80 pounds.

As soon as Jay took the gear off, he fell to the ground.

He looked like he died.

I yelled, "Get the NARCAN."

Now, if you don't know what NARCAN is, NARCAN is actually an antidote that fights opioid overdose.

Later on, we found out that the suspect was actually using heroin mixed with fentanyl.

Fentanyl is an opioid that, at that time, was a huge problem within the entire United States. Hundreds of thousands of people were dying from overdosing on Fentanyl. Our bodies were not used to the substance, and the suspect was able to function normally. But when the substance made contact with Jay and the team, which I was light-headed during that moment, I had to think fast.

Luckily, a month and a half before that operation, my Sergeant had shipped me out to the Drug Enforcement Administration (DEA) Academy in Quantico, Virginia.

During my training at the DEA Academy, I learned how to handle critical situations, just like what happened during the operation.

Within seconds, I yelled to the other detectives, "Get the NARCAN. Jay is possibly exposed to fentanyl." The team then placed the actual antidote, the NARCAN, inside of Jay's nostrils, and we sprayed the NARCAN nasal spray. We did two nasal sprays; he was still not waking up. The third nasal spray revived Jay. His eyes were wide open, and he took a big deep breath. He almost died that day. And all I could remember was the conversation that me and Jay had earlier that day. He had told me that he had a surprise for his longtime girlfriend, whom he wanted to marry in Las Vegas that weekend. And he almost died… He got sent to the hospital.

"Paul, you're going to be a commander one day. You're in charge of this operation now. We're going to go to the hospital to check on Jay," said my Lieutenant.

Let's stop and think about how crazy the last few years of my life have been since I became a cop. Life can change so fast within a few years. I was a detective at that time with almost three and a half years of experience taking charge of an operation with law enforcement detectives who had 10 - 15 years of experience, and I was running the show based on my leadership. It doesn't matter how long you've been in any niche, industry, or profession. Everyone is different. You can surpass anyone if you put double the effort into anything. Remember that.

After the incident happened, I remember driving home, and the chief of police for my police agency called me. And this is the first time I've actually talked to the chief of police at this time. The chief of police told me, "Paul, we heard what happened. We're happy you're alive. Do you need to take some time off for yourself?" I didn't think much of it. I didn't think of the situation that could have potentially killed me, killed my coworker, or endangered everyone else on my team. It was almost like I was jaded. I didn't know how to feel. I told the chief of police, "No, thank you. I have to head into the office early tomorrow morning at 6 AM. I want to get this case charged against that suspect, the narcotic trafficker that almost killed my partner."

From that day, it changed my mindset completely. It changed my mindset where I really looked into my life. I was devoting 60 to 100-hour work weeks to a profession that did fulfill me, but at what cost? I wasn't seeing my family. I was losing myself to the profession. My personal relationship with my ex-girlfriend at that time was just getting worse and worse, and we eventually separated because we didn't spend enough time together.

My ex and I would get into consistent arguments because she would always tell me, "You're always working." "You're never home." "You only care about yourself." I didn't know what to do at this point in my life, but I knew that I needed to change my situation.

CHAPTER 2

Developing a Millionaire's Mindset

Now, before we get into my transition from a high-speed narcotics detective in one of the most dangerous cities in the United States to a striving entrepreneur building bootstrap startups and creating different opportunities that help thousands of aspiring entrepreneurs create another form of income, let's briefly talk about a millionaire's mindset.

What creates a successful person? Is it your environment? Is it the school you went to? Is it your upbringing? I always ask myself this question every year, especially on my birthdays.

As I got older, I always made a promise to myself: this year would be different. As I got older and as I got to experience my share of successful business ventures and failed ventures, I realized that your mindset plays a significant role in determining your own life outcome. Nothing else is to blame for your own success besides what you believe is meant for you in life. If you believe you will become a millionaire, then you must believe you are a millionaire and work like you are a millionaire.

Remember, you cannot be a millionaire and have a minimum-wage work mentality.

It's you versus you.

Make it happen for yourself.

Dealing with negativity. Ever had an idea, goal, or dream that you were always so excited to express to a close family member, spouse, or friend? Just to have them tell you every possible bad thing that can go wrong with your idea? For example, when I wanted to transition from being a sales manager in corporate America to working in law enforcement, I told my ex-girlfriend of seven years at the time, and she laughed. "Yeah, right. You can't be a cop," she stated.

A few years later, on the day of my police academy graduation, my ex-girlfriend made a speech at my graduation dinner with my family and friends stating how she always believed in me and knew I would be a police officer. When I told my coworkers in the police academy that I would love to become a detective later on in my law enforcement career, my coworkers stated, "You barely passed the academy. Good luck." Well, a few years later, I was awarded top detective out of twelve police agencies with numerous accommodations. My coworkers then stated, "Paul's going to be the police chief one day."

Or how about when I started my side hustle with my first ATM while working in law enforcement and telling my parents about the ATM business? My parents questioned me and thought it was a waste of time. My mother stated, "You are a detective. Study to become a police sergeant and forget about anything else. You have great benefits." Well, a few years later, I left my 9 to 5 job, building multiple companies that have generated over $22 million across all my ventures. My parents are now proud and always ask what I'm working on next.

You see, people always doubt you and your ability to get the job done, and that's okay. One thing you have to realize is that if you allow the negative statements, the negative ideas, or the negative mindset to overpower what you believe you can achieve, then you will never be able to be successful in life. As you can see, I didn't write the chain of events above to brag about my life. I wrote them to show you that no matter what you tell someone, it's natural for them to think of the bad first. It's human nature. People are afraid of the unknown and what makes them uncomfortable.

Life is too short, and we're all here for a limited time. Make sure to regret nothing in life and take risks to achieve anything that is meant for you. Negatives will just slow you down during your journey in life. You must not allow negativity to win. You are a winner and must win at all costs.

I keep my circle small. As you grow as a person, a professional, or an entrepreneur, you will start noticing a significant change in your social environment. People will approach you for different reasons, and your time and your resources will become even more valuable. Keeping a small circle of friends can be an essential strategy for maintaining your sanity and focusing on what truly matters. Quality over quantity.

It is important to surround yourself with people who provide value to your life. The group of friends that I had in my early 20s is completely different from the group of friends that I have in my early 30s. Why? I wanted more in life in my 20s. I wanted a better career. I wanted better experiences and a better lifestyle. My friends at the time were comfortable with working their current jobs, which were barely covering their monthly bills. And the majority of them wanted to party every weekend. Trust me, I had my fair share of fun in my 20s as well as being a nightclub promoter and reminiscing about the spontaneous weekend trips to Vegas with my friends. But after a while, the parties and that lifestyle get really old.

I needed a better influence from the people around me. I started to network with coworkers at my corporate sales job at the time, and I got to know the top sales producers and what made them good at their job.

I would then duplicate the methods and strategies that worked for them and made them successful.

I did the exact same thing when I joined law enforcement. I hung around the best police officers who were high achievers in my department and would become friends with the best investigators to figure out what made them successful.

When I became a full-time entrepreneur, I would introduce myself to other entrepreneurs at business conferences that I knew were highly successful in their industry and figure out what worked for them and if I could apply their methods to my life. Many making friends with high achievers is a cheat code that no one speaks about. It's actually one of the fastest methods to get you where you want to go the fastest. Surround yourself with the right people.

A great benefit of you becoming your own boss is that you can employ your family and friends. On the journey to the top, you can give opportunities to other people who were there at pivotal times in your life and gave you motivation to move ahead.

Since we are at the part of the book where I'm giving you guys real-life examples of how I think dealing with negativity and choosing to surround yourself with, I want to share the story of how I met my Chief Operating Officer of one of my companies, ATMTogether.com.

Gedam. I met Gedam while working in law enforcement. Gedam was always an outgoing and disciplined police officer. He was very different from the other officers because he was always trying to take his career to the next level. Gedam became one of the youngest Sergeants in my department with only five years on the job.

At that time, I had already established my ATM business with 30 locations throughout California and had just launched my online business, ATMTogether.com. Gedam would always stop by my office, where I was assigned to talk about the growth of my businesses and his interest in how business worked. Gedam was also a fellow investor just like me, and Gedam was able to become a millionaire from the crazy growth that happened with Bitcoin within the past few years. Gedam had also invested in a few ATMs as a silent investor.

As my businesses were growing, I remember one day coming into the office excited because I had just cleared my third month of running ATMTogether.com as a one-man entrepreneur and clearing over $130,000 in revenue in a single month. At this point, my tangible ATM business was covering my monthly living expenses, and I was able to save extra cash. My net worth was over $1 million dollars. My new online business, ATMtogether.com, made me about one year's worth of my job's salary.

Yet, I was hesitant to leave my job that I worked extremely hard to get, and I just needed confirmation that leaving my job was a good idea. I had a conversation with my mother at the time, and I asked her, "Mom, I think I should leave law enforcement for good and focus on growing this new online business I just created. What do you think?"

My mother replied, "You have to remember that your job gives you great benefits, and you should at least make $1 million dollars from your new business before leaving your job."

In the back of my mind, I respected my mom's advice, but I always knew that my mother was never in this type of situation before. Throughout my time in law enforcement, I was tempted to build rapport with coworkers around my intentions of building wealth, investments, etc. I recalled multiple times that coworkers would not like to discuss anything that was not law enforcement related, which made it difficult to build trust with most of my peers.

That same day that I went into the office and was happy about generating the revenue from my business, Gedam had stopped by the office, and I showed him my merchant processing account, which showed him my total revenue for the month that I made from ATMTogether.com. Gedam stated, "Bro, what are you still doing here? Leave and grow your new company."

That was it. That was the confirmation that I needed to hear. The very next day, I submitted my two weeks' notice to my department. The rumors that I was leaving spread like fire, and I had over 100 officers stop by my office for the next few weeks. People would wonder and ask what department I was transferring to or if I was applying to work for the federal government. When I would tell each one of my coworkers that I was leaving law enforcement for good because a couple of my businesses were going well, the response was surprising. Some coworkers would congratulate me, but most were at a loss for words in an awkward, standoffish manner.

The same week, I contacted my real estate agent, and I sold my house. I decided I needed a change. I decided to move to San Diego, California, from the San Francisco Bay Area to be around a new environment and also to focus on growing ATMTogether.com. A couple of days before I left the department, I had asked Gedam if he would ever leave law enforcement. "Paul, if I had the opportunity to do what you are doing, then I would leave without thinking. You are going to live the American dream. You're going to be your own boss," said Gedam.

At that time, it was a very unique situation for me because making money online was very new to me, and I had to figure out how to grow the company.

Since Gedam was one of the few people that I knew was interested in business from my actual department, I asked Gedam if he would like to work part-time for me. He agreed and started on a part-time basis whenever he was not working as a police sergeant.

As ATMTogether.com grew, I needed to hire full-time employees, and I offered Gedam a commission-based position in my organization, where he had the potential to make up to $20,000 a month. Gedam eventually left the police department and joined ATMTogether.com full-time as a consultant. Eventually, Gedam was promoted to an executive position as Chief Operating Officer, where he managed over 50 employees and now makes more than double what he was making as a police sergeant.

As I expanded into merchant services (Credit Card Machines) and other business opportunities, which I will cover in the next chapters, I offered Gedam the opportunity to become co-owner of one of my other companies, which is called MerchantAutomation.com.

Gedam left law enforcement and had zero knowledge of digital marketing or running a multimillion-dollar company. He was able to successfully run multiple businesses and learn how to become an expert digital marketer due to being flexible with working in almost every position in the company and willing to learn every day. The day you stop learning is the day you stop growing.

When you have good people that you can trust and are loyal around you, make sure to take them with you to the top. It takes a tribe to build a sustainable business especially after you make $10 million dollars in revenue. Let's take a step back into how I was able to build my first ATM Business before ATMTogether.com in the next chapter.

CHAPTER 3

The ATM Side Hustle

Back in 2018, I had left the Narcotics Task Force and was transferred to the Special Victims Unit as a Detective. I was working late one day, and one of my co-workers, who was a 15-year veteran police officer, stopped by to ask questions about a case I was working on. We will call him Sonny for the purposes of this chapter.

"Paul, are you investing in anything currently?" stated Sonny.

"I'm actually looking for a side hustle right now. I'm actually trying to find a way to become financially free," I stated.

So we started talking, and as we started talking, he mentioned Automated Teller Machines (ATMs).

During our conversation, Sonny said, "Did you know that you can actually own those ATMs that you see at the gas stations, convenience stores, nail salons, essentially everywhere?"

I always thought the bank owned ATMs, I thought to myself.

When I heard this idea, I remember being in disbelief. *It's so simple, and it makes sense!*

I remember questioning Sonny if he had any machines or even started the business himself. He said he'd actually known about the ATM business for quite a few years, except he'd been stuck on analysis paralysis.

Sonny was afraid to take the leap, but he loved the idea!

If you don't know what analysis paralysis is, it's essentially when you find an idea or an opportunity, and you research and research and research because you're scared of the risk, and you don't move forth at all, but you have all of this knowledge built up and you continue to research to find a certain answer that will make you feel better to actually take the first step.

I did my due diligence; I went online, I researched as much as I could, and I executed.

I remember reaching out to multiple manufacturers that sold ATMs. I saw two common ATM models everywhere.

The first one was called the Hyosung Halo II.

The second model was the Genmega G2500.

I ended up going with a big ATM corporation that actually ended up selling me six ATMs at a discounted rate.

At that time, I had purchased the ATMs for roughly around $2,100. I also signed up with them for their processing network.

If you don't know what the processing network is, the processing network is the network that facilitates the card transactions through your ATM, which connects your ATM to the banking network and then connects your ATM to your actual business checking account.

As an owner of an Automated Teller Machine (ATM), you make money each time a customer uses your ATM to take out cash.

A convenience fee or charge is placed on the machine, and you collect that fee.

You are paid on a daily basis the cash you placed in your ATM and the fee, which is directly deposited into your business bank account daily.

Think about yourself being a private money lender for the general public and lending your own cash to customers and the customers paying you for letting the customers borrow your cash.

The cash you let the customer borrow is then deposited back into your bank account along with the fee you charged the customer.

Your cash is working for you instead of sitting in your savings account. This is called PASSIVE income. *The ATM does all of the work for you!*

It's a very simple business. I ended up signing a three-year contract with this large distributor of ATMs. Along with that, they took a large portion of my surcharge fees, which later on in the story, you're going to learn to never do.

From the time that I spoke with my coworker, I executed and landed locations. Within two weeks, I had landed six locations to place my ATMs. The reason why I was able to do this very quickly was simply because I had sales experience in corporate America before I was in law enforcement. All I simply did was take some vacation time, took about two weeks, and went out to door knock and cold call on small businesses that were cash-driven or incentivized to use cash. Even if locations had established ATMs, I still spoke with the business owners and saw what value I could provide that their current ATM deployer was not providing. I must have gone through hundreds of businesses, and I was able to land six locations. A few of them were in liquor stores, a few of them were nail salons, and a couple of them were in barber shops.

I remember the day that I actually installed these ATMs. I was very excited. I thought to myself, this is it. This is the change that I need in my life. This is what's going to get me financially free.

After two months of having the actual machines inside of these six locations, only three of the ATMs were generating profit. The other three ATMs barely made me $50. I remember being angry. I remember being sad. I remember saying, "This is too good to be true. I knew it." Then I remembered that if everything was easy, then everyone would do it. I went back online, I did more research and some more research. I finally joined Facebook after not being on social media for eight years. I remember joining multiple ATM-related Facebook groups. The great thing about Facebook groups is that you're able to actually see and network with other like-minded individuals just like yourself, just like me. This is why later on, as you read this book, you're going to learn why I created one of the largest Facebook groups online called ATM Business for Beginners, with currently 66,000 members.

While I was in these Facebook groups, I actually networked with a seasoned ATM entrepreneur out of Southern California. I remember I sent him a message through Facebook and introduced myself, letting him know that I had just started the business and that half of my ATMs were not producing the profits that I thought were going to produce. Well, we jumped on a phone call, and after talking to him for several weeks, I finally asked him if he could become my mentor. He said, "Yes!"

The first thing that he told me was to get out of the three-year contract with the ATM company that I had signed up originally with. The reason why is that he said, as a new ATM deployer, you shouldn't have to give any of your surcharge profits to anyone, and you shouldn't have to sign any contract. You should be able to leave at any time. This is the reason why several companies out there will give you a large discounted rate when you first buy the machines.

So, if you are brand new and you're even interested in investing in ATMs, there are two very important tips that I could give you as you read my story. Make sure that you never give any of your surcharge profits to anyone. You should keep 100% of your profits. Number two, don't sign a contract for your processing network.

As the weeks went by, I listened to my mentor. He showed me strategies on how to get better leads, to negotiate better, and to market my business to potential prospects. By the third month of being in the ATM industry, I had relocated three of my ATMs, which I like to call floating assets. I call them floating assets because if your ATM doesn't work in one location, you could always relocate it to another location, and it will produce better results for you.

This is why I am such a big believer in the ATM business, even in 2023.

If one location doesn't work out, you can always move the same ATM.

By the end of the third month, I had relocated my ATMs, and I could generate $3,000 in semi-passive income from those six ATMs. I still remember thinking to myself, if I gave up before I met my mentor, I would have actually lost a lot of profit.

The day I saw the $3,000 dollars in residuals in my bank account, I told myself, I can grow this simple business, and I can do this while still working my nine to five. It's possible.

Fifteen months later, I had over 30 locations that would profit me anywhere between $12,000 to $15,000 in residual income from my ATMs. I was able to land multiple deals from different business owners who were referred by my mentor. I even had locations that were making me $1,500 net profit from a single ATM. If I can do this, you can do this as well. It all comes down to your mindset.

I was able to become financially free, and I had my side hustle to cover my bills.

A few things changed ever since I became financially free at that time.

Number one, I didn't have to worry about my bills anymore.

Number two, I didn't have to work overtime anymore.

Number three, I had less stress.

Number four, I was able to use the active income from law enforcement, and I was able to invest it into either other ventures or other investments.

I remember I had saved up quite a bit of money.

And I remember I used to daydream for the past eight years about this car.

One day, I was sitting at my desk, and I was thinking, should I grow my ATM business even more, or should I diversify and look at other avenues now that my ATMs have freed my time?

And during that time, I made the decision. I needed something to encourage me to scale my business. I needed to reward myself. For the past five years, at this time, I had worked anywhere between 60 to 100-hour work weeks. Not only that, but I was also able to have a relationship. I was able to juggle spending time with my family, taking vacations with my family, and also creating a five-figure-a-month business on the side. It came all from time management, being disciplined, and having the mindset.

I purchased my dream vehicle, a Porsche Panamera. The next day, I drove to work in my brand new car.

As I pulled up to the employee parking lot of the police station, I remember there were several of my coworkers, even a couple of supervisors that were talking among themselves. They were just standing there in awe, looking at my vehicle, looking at that brand new Porsche Panamera, wondering whose car that was.

Through the grapevine, a couple of friends of mine stopped by the office, and they were like, "Hey, Paul, everyone's saying that you got a new Porsche Panamera. There's even a supervisor saying I wonder how he's able to afford that on a cop's salary, and you more than likely sell drugs on the side."

See, not everybody knew that I had a side hustle. Nobody knew that I had a business when I was in law enforcement. I was very low key. I'm a big believer in accomplishing your goals first and then talking about it. I've never been a big talker. When I had that car, it made me feel like a boss. It made me feel like I could do anything. It's just simply because I had wanted that vehicle for the past eight years. It was something that many of my family members, a lot of my friends, and even my coworkers said was out of reach for me.

But I was able to do it.

As I went on and I continued to work in law enforcement, and I continued to be an entrepreneur with ATMs, my mindset just grew to the possibilities we all have in life. I wanted to learn more. One day, I was actually talking to a coworker, and I started expanding into different social media platforms like Instagram, Twitter, and YouTube.

Remember, guys, I wasn't on social media for eight years, but you know how social media platforms work—Facebook is always listening. As I was talking to my coworker, I was telling him about how successful entrepreneurs online were showing other regular people just like me, just like you, how to become successful entrepreneurs just like them.

During this time, I had a very successful ATM business. It transformed from a side hustle with a couple of ATMs to a very successful business while I was still working my nine-to-five. I told my coworker, "I think I can do that. I think I can go ahead and show the average Joe, just like me, how to start a side hustle with ATMs and become financially free and have the option to leave their nine to five if they would like to."

See, at that time, I wasn't thinking about leaving my nine-to-five job because I genuinely loved law enforcement. I loved being a cop. I loved being a detective. That was me. It fulfilled me. I didn't do it for the money. We got paid well, but I didn't do it for the money. I did it for the cause.

As I sat down at my desk and I was looking through Facebook, I saw an ad. The ad was promoting a book about digital marketing. The book was free, and all I had to do was pay shipping costs, which was $5 dollars. I ordered the book and got it within a few days. I remember sitting down when I had free time at work and reading this book. This book was amazing. It actually opened my eyes to the opportunities of what is possible online with starting a digital marketing company.

I remember calling the company that had written the book; they had a program that showed people like myself, just like you, how to start an online education business. So, if you were an expert in your niche, you knew more than the average person, then you can build a program and actually sell it online. After jumping on a call with a consultant from this company and investing $10,000 in self-education from them, I embarked on my journey of starting a program to show others how to successfully start their own ATM business.

Now, later on in the book, I am going to go into more detail about digital marketing in the online space, how it works, and how I can help you do exactly what I did. But for now, let's just stick to ATMs. I also want to give you a FREE gift before you finish this chapter!

It's an EBook called "2023 Blueprint on how to build your own ATM business."

You can download it here: ATMTogether.com/ATMBluePrint

This PDF will break down step by step how to set up an entire ATM business and have you up and running within the next 30 days! Make sure to put this valuable information to use!

As I grew ATMTogether.com within the past three years and having over 2,600 clients under the ATMtogether.com brand, I was able to network and be introduced to several entrepreneurs who are highly successful in the ATM industry.

Towards the end of 2022, I met an extremely successful entrepreneur in the ATM industry who had reached out to me on social media. He wanted to talk to me about a business opportunity. Well, the business opportunity, if you guys have been researching my company ATMTogether.com, it had to do with Bitcoin ATMs.

As we were talking, he was a highly successful entrepreneur in the ATM industry and had hundreds of ATMs across the nation, but he focused on building the infrastructure and fulfillment to launch a business where we can help anyone who's interested in investing in Bitcoin ATMs.

Now, if you're not familiar with Bitcoin ATMs, let me explain exactly how it works. Let's talk about Bitcoin. Bitcoin, for the last few years, has fluctuated in price, anywhere between $20,000 up to $60,000. Now, think of you as being a broker. You end up purchasing a machine (BTM) that facilitates the buys and sales of Bitcoin. The biggest difference between someone using the Bitcoin machine and using an online exchange is the wait time. When you use an online exchange, you have to wait a few days to receive your funds. With a Bitcoin machine, it's within a few minutes. The minute that you hit buy or sell, you get your funds automatically. It's for convenience.

Nowadays, people want everything instantly since COVID made the general public want everything quickly. Being the owner of a BTM, you receive commissions off of every buy and sell of a Bitcoin, which makes this very lucrative. The Crypto will have a markup of 15-20% for your customers. Basically, for every $1,000 dollars of crypto purchased, you will make around $150 dollars in profits from the crypto sale. If 1 transaction occurs for 1 Bitcoin worth $25,000 from your BTM, then you would make around $3,750 from that 1 transaction. Imagine having 2-5 transactions monthly. It's possible!

This changed my belief in crypto. In the past, I was not a big fan of crypto. I was scared. I didn't understand it. But once I did my due diligence, I researched, I started researching more and more about it. I saw that it was a very low risk when it came to owning the Bitcoin ATMs. This entrepreneur and I became business partners. And that's when I invested in my first three BTMs.

I'm a big believer in doing good business. If I'm going to sell anything to anyone, I'm going to bring social proof first. I'm going to go ahead and actually do it myself, bring the results, and then show you that it's possible to do. And that's exactly what I did.

By January of 2023, my company launched the first and only program that actually helps investors purchase their own Bitcoin machine. Not only that, but we actually facilitate absolutely everything. And it's a game changer because now someone who lives in Florida can deploy as many Bitcoin ATMs throughout the United States and potentially make thousands of dollars monthly from their own BTM remotely and passively.

As I was growing up, I was never taught about financial freedom. I was taught about the American dream. The American dream was to go to school, get accepted to college, get a college degree, get a good-paying job, buy a house, have kids, have a family, and that's it. Work your 40 years, retire, have a good retirement, and enjoy life. Go on vacation. There's nothing wrong with that idea. But I was always a big believer in why we have to work 40 years or more to retire. Why can't we just expedite that process? Create multiple streams of income for yourself and retire early, retire 30 years earlier? That has been my mindset for the past decade.

I had to learn from personal experience, from self-education, from changing my circle to learn what true financial freedom is. True financial freedom is not having a good job that makes six, seven figures, but you're actively working for that income. Financial freedom is having your assets pay you so you can enjoy the time to do whatever you want, whether it's to work on another business or to go ahead and actually spend time with your family. That is the true definition of financial freedom: either work less or not work at all and make the same amount of cash flow monthly.

I learned this the hard way. I come from corporate America, working more than 100 hours as a sales manager. I come from law enforcement, where I was working anywhere between 60 to 100 hours a week, working, sleeping three hours a day, and working an 18-hour shift. I've experienced both sides. And what I can tell you is once you invest and make money while you are sleeping, it will change your life. Everybody makes an active income. If you have a job, it doesn't matter what job you have, you are making an active income. You are trading your time for money. But what if I were to tell you there was a way to make money while you're not working? What would you call that? It's actually called passive income. And like I was saying before, passive income is what is going to be the needle mover in your life. That is what's going to get you financially free. Most people think that in real estate, that is true passive income. But in reality, it is not. If you get a rental property, you still have to manage your tenants. You still have to manage remodeling the home, fixing the homes, and managing the homes.

But if you invest in a fully automated business where you do not do anything and receive funds at the end of the month, that's what I call passive income. That's essentially what I was able to turn my ATM business and my BTM business into. ATMs are not 100% passive in the beginning. The way you are able to make ATMs fully passive is if you hire a team or employees to actually manage and refill the machines with cash. That's what I was able to do after my 15th ATM. With a BTM, my employees take care of absolutely everything, which makes it passive. If you want to be financially free, you have to figure out a way to make your money work for you while you're able to either focus on your main source of income or diversify your funds to make it work for you to create that passive income.

If Bitcoin ATMs caught your attention, then I want to provide more VALUE to you. Here is another FREE pdf called "2023 BluePrint with Bitcoin ATMs."

Go Here: ATMTogether.com/BTMBluePrint to download!

This PDF will give you a step-by-step game plan on what you need to do in order to get your first BTM up and running. Good luck and Execute!

CHAPTER 4

The Credit Card Machine Business

Merchant services, also known as the credit card machine business, is a set of tools and services that allows any business to accept payments from customers in various ways, especially through credit cards and debit cards.

Here's how it works in simple terms:

1. A customer decides to buy something from a store.

2. The customer can choose to pay with a credit card, debit card, or sometimes even with a smartphone.

3. The business uses a terminal, a credit card machine, or software provided by the merchant services company to process the payment.

4. The merchant services network communicates with the customer's bank to make sure that they have enough money or credit.

5. If everything is okay, the payment gets approved, and the money is eventually transferred from the customer's bank account to the business's bank account.

6. The merchant services company takes a small fee for helping with this process.

7. So, merchant services basically help business owners collect payments smoothly and securely without dealing only with cash.

In late 2022, I was introduced to two entrepreneurs named Rob and John out of Los Angeles, California.

To give you some background on Rob and John, they own a merchant services company slash independent sales organization. They've been in the merchant services industry for the past 18 years and have generated over $170 million in revenue from their merchant services company. On top of that, they are also serial entrepreneurs who own a large amount of real estate and are experts in the Airbnb business.

Two of my business partners from the ATM industry, Lee and Mike, were at a business conference and befriended Rob. During the conversation, Rob showed Lee a Facebook group on his phone called ATM Business for Beginners and asked Lee if he knew about this specific Facebook group. Lee responded with, "Yes, that's Paul's group." Lee and Mike invited me to a meeting with Rob and John, who were interested in speaking with me.

During the meeting, Rob and John explained how this new program that has been out for the past few years, called the Cash Discount Program, works and how there is a big opportunity to create another source of passive income through this program currently in the United States.

The cash discount program is a way for businesses like stores or restaurants to give a special price to customers who pay with cash.

Here's how it works in simple steps:

1. The business decides that they want to encourage people to pay with cash instead of credit cards because when people pay with cards, the business usually has to pay a small fee to the credit card company. I have seen companies pay anywhere between $300 up to thousands of dollars monthly for this merchant services service.

2. To do this, the business must raise their regular prices a little bit. These higher prices are what customers pay if they use a credit card.

3. But if a customer pays with cash, the business gives them a discount. So they pay less than the credit card price. This lower price is close to what the original price was before the little increase.

4. Basically, the cash discount program is like saying, "Hey, if you want to pay with cash, you have a special deal, and you pay a little less." It's a way for businesses to save on the fees they pay to credit card companies and share some of the savings with

customers who pay in cash. It's a win-win for the merchant and for the merchant services company providing the cash discount program. The merchant services company still gets paid residuals from the percentage that is charged and paid for by the consumer.

I decided to start my own merchant services company to use the cash discount program as my primary offer for business owners. By the end of June of 2023, I was able to acquire over 60 merchant accounts myself throughout the United States and switch them over to utilizing the cash discount program that's generating over $20,000 in monthly residuals for my new merchant services company and saving 100% of the fees for the business owners. It was a win-win. This was massive and a huge eye-opener for me.

This was another simple business that I was able to execute with the resources and knowledge of building my prior startups.

I decided to launch an online program called MerchantAutomation.com, which is essentially a merchant services business in a box. My company helps clients get into the merchant services business, providing them with their first merchant account, terminal installation, and any additional resources they may need to continue their business.

Since I have access to the processing network due to the partnership with Ron and John, I figured I could help entrepreneurs across the United States expand into this industry as well. We can grow faster together and essentially become business partners with the residual splits!

Since the start of MerchantAutomation.com, I was able to generate over $2.5 million in revenue within eight months.

Within eight months, my company has enrolled over 160 clients, with dozens of success stories of clients generating anywhere between $200 to $1200 dollars in monthly residuals from their first merchant account with my company.

The merchant services industry is a big blue ocean with a ton of opportunity, as there are millions of businesses out there that do not use the cash discount program yet, and merchants are paying thousands of dollars in fees monthly.

Only about 5% of all business owners in the United States currently use the cash discount program, which is a MASSIVE opportunity for anyone who is willing to execute.

Merchant services, aka the credit card machine business, is going to be one of the best forms of semi-to-passive income along with ATMs and BTMs. You can set it up and forget it.

If you want to learn more, then I want to give you another gift! Here is a FREE Course called "The Cash Discount Program BluePrint."

Go Here to Access: MerchantAutomation.com/MerchantBluePrint

I hope you take advantage of the course and further educate yourself in this great opportunity to build residual income for you and your family!

CHAPTER 5

Self Education and Digital Marketing

I stopped using social media around the age of 22 years old. The last time I was on social media was during the Myspace era. Do you remember when you would create a page and have background music? Good times, huh? I was scrolling through Facebook one day while I was working at the office, and I noticed that there were a few entrepreneurs promoting their expertise and selling courses or programs to the general public, which I found very interesting.

The last time I was on social media, I did not remember anyone trying to sell anything. I always thought social media was about connecting with others and seeing what their day was about. The more and more I started researching courses and programs on ATMs, I noticed that every single person who was promoting a course or a program had barely any experience within the ATM industry, which I found odd because I thought ATMs were such a simple business that a good program or course would skyrocket to the mass online.

As weeks and even months passed by, I found myself reading more and more about different businesses online like, Amazon automation,

Forex trading, real estate wholesaling, and digital marketing consulting. One day I told myself, *I'm going to do it myself. I'm just going to start a course about my expertise in the ATM business.* I didn't know how to start or where to even begin. I wanted to see what the other ATM gurus were providing in their programs.

I ended up spending thousands of dollars to purchase several ATM courses. I was actually shocked. The three courses that I purchased provided the bone stock minimum resources and information needed to launch your own ATM business. Hardly any value and not to be negative towards anyone else, but I could see why selling a course online has a bad rap. Imagine spending a few hundred or even thousands of dollars for a course that you thought would help you establish a business that might potentially change your life or give you the skills to execute a business. But you end up with a few videos that provide you with basic information that you could have found for free on YouTube. Trust me, I would be angry too.

I knew there was a major opportunity to really showcase my skills and provide value to the general public about starting their own ATM business as a side hustle, which would make it a no-brainer offer. My thought process was that ATMs were a black and white business that didn't require a ton of time and that anyone could do this part-time. I really wanted to help the average person who was working a nine-to-five and was looking for a way out. Even though I was working 60 to 100-hour work weeks with all the additional overtime shifts that I was working, I was able to successfully launch my own ATM business and scale my ATM business to additional figures monthly. I also noticed that

I was very relatable compared to a lot of the online gurus that I observed while going and searching through Facebook.

A lot of the online gurus were in their younger 20s and didn't really have that much life experience based on what they would say about their life online. I was approaching my 30s and had a ton of life experience. I was a successful detective in law enforcement. I successfully launched and grew my own ATM business as a side hustle as well. And lastly, I had the right mindset and intent to provide so much value about the ATM industry that anyone who did not buy my program would feel dumb for not doing so.

I know the next thing I'm going to tell you is going to sound cliche, but this is as real as it gets. And it all started with a book on digital marketing. You're probably thinking, *Paul, really? A book?* Yes, it actually started with a book. I spent about $5 on a book called *Digital Millionaire*.

I'm going to be honest with you: I'm not a reader, but I read this book within four hours and then read it another two times for clarity purposes. This book explained how an average guy who had lost everything from owning his own bar, who actually shared the same foundations as me, was able to sell his expertise during an online webinar and made tens of thousands of dollars within one hour of just selling information. Now, for most people, they would automatically assume this guy was full of shit. But to me, all I read was an *opportunity*. It was amazing.

The following week, I signed up for my first online course, which cost about $10,000. I know you're probably thinking, *Paul, seriously? $10,000 for a course? Are you crazy?* The course taught you the foundations of digital marketing, like creating a clear offer to your audience and how to build the infrastructure of an online business.

This was around April 2020, and I was still working at the police department and managing my ATM portfolio. I still remember reviewing a few of the course videos, and one of the other detectives who had just walked by my desk asked me, "Hey, Paul, what are you looking at?"

I told him, "This program that I just purchased for $10,000 on how to start a digital marketing business.

He laughed and said, "Get real, bro. You can't make any serious money from being an influencer."

I said nothing. I didn't let it bother me. At the end of the day, that was nothing new to me. Others will always stay comfortable if that's all they know. So, I went back to watching the videos at my desk and focused on learning the process of being a digital marketer. There had to be literally over 100 hours worth of content in this program, and it took me several weeks to really understand everything.

The process that worked best for me was this:

- I reviewed each training video without taking notes, absorbing the information.

- Then, I watched the same training video twice and started taking action step by step while noting down what the video taught me.

By September 2020, I officially launched my first online program, 30DayATMBiz.com. While it may not have been the flashiest name, it focused on helping aspiring entrepreneurs start their ATM business within 30 days.

I didn't know much about running Facebook ads or digital consulting, and I was stepping into a completely new world. However, armed with determination, the right mindset, and a strong work ethic, I devised a simple game plan to find potential clients and convert them into paying customers.

Here's how it went:

1. I started selling my program for $997.00 online.

2. I created a Facebook group called "ATM Business for Beginners" to attract potential clients.

3. In this group, I provided valuable information for free, including guides and a mini-course to introduce people to the basics of the ATM business.

4. The goal was to build rapport and trust with group members over time.

5. I conducted weekly live training sessions within the group to interact with members, sharing my journey and insights into the ATM business.

6. To expand my group, I engaged in other Facebook groups with similar interests, such as vending machines, car rental, and real estate investing groups.

7. I provided value in these groups and engaged in private conversations with members, mentioning my "ATM Business for Beginners" group.

Within two months, my Facebook group grew to 1,000 members. I dedicated my mornings, from 5 AM to 1 PM, to messaging group members, creating posts with valuable information, and engaging with group members.

By September 2020, I had made my first $3,000 in course sales in a single month, and by November 2020, I had reached $6,000. While I was pleased with the results, I knew I could achieve more. I saw claims from other digital marketers making $100,000 monthly and believed I could do it, too.

I invested an additional $7,000 in another digital marketing program to learn different techniques, strategies, and how to scale my online business. This was a significant portion of my profits, and I hadn't yet recouped my original $10,000 investment.

However, I was determined to make this venture successful and believed in my abilities. I committed fully to the journey.

In December 2020, after speaking with many aspiring entrepreneurs, I identified a common challenge in the ATM business: finding locations. To address this pain point and provide more value, I pivoted and changed the program's name from 30DayATMBiz.com to ATMTogether.com.

ATMTogether.com's Automation program offered not just a course but also tangible elements like an ATM, a location, internet access, the processing network, customer service support, technical training, and unlimited wholesale pricing for additional ATMs and locations. This hybrid offer aimed to simplify success.

AN ATM BUSINESS BUILT BY US FOR YOU

Fast forward to January 2021, three days after my birthday, I made the first sale for the new ATMTogether.com program at $6,000. By

March 2023, I had generated over $130,000 in revenue in a single month, all while managing this digital company, working as a detective, and overseeing my ATM business alone. It was a time of immense personal transformation and growth.

How to Build a 7-Figure Company Online From My Experience

Building a seven-figure digital company requires a blend of strategic planning, dedication, and execution. While there's no guaranteed path to success, the following steps were the ones I took to build my online companies:

Niche Selection:

Start by defining a clear niche or target market. Do you want to serve e-commerce businesses, local businesses, startups, or specific industries? Niching down can help you tailor your services and messaging and make you stand out.

Build a Solid Brand:

- **Name:** Choose a memorable name that aligns with your business values and offerings.

- **Logo & Visual Identity:** Create a consistent look and feel across all channels.

- **Unique Selling Proposition (USP):** Clearly define what makes you different from competitors.

Continuously improve and update your knowledge and skills in these areas.

Pricing Strategy:

Decide on your pricing model. Will you use a retainer-based model, project-based, or performance-based pricing? The right model can greatly affect your revenue potential.

Sales & Lead Generation:

- Develop a sales funnel and automate where possible using CRM systems.

- Use lead magnets, webinars, and other content marketing strategies to attract potential clients.

- Consider partnerships with complementary businesses to exchange referrals.

Quality Deliverables:

Always prioritize quality over quantity. Delivering outstanding results will earn you repeat business and referrals.

Client Retention:

It's often easier and more cost-effective to retain existing clients than to acquire new ones. Focus on exceptional customer service, regular communication, and always over-deliver.

Expand:

As you establish your business:

- Scale your team by hiring specialists or expanding your services.
- Expand your clientele by targeting larger businesses or diversifying your target market.

Digital Presence:

- Have a user-friendly, modern website showcasing your services, case studies, testimonials, and more.
- Engage in content marketing. Share your expertise through posts, videos, podcasts, and more.
- Utilize social media platforms relevant to your business.

Network:

- Join digital marketing communities, forums, and attend conferences. Networking can open doors to collaborations, partnerships, and client leads.

Stay Updated:

The digital marketing landscape is constantly evolving. Ensure that you and your team stay updated with the latest trends, tools, and technologies.

Invest in Tools and Technology:

Leverage digital marketing tools that can help streamline your processes and provide better results for clients. This includes SEO tools, PPC management tools, social media management tools, and more.

Financial Management:

- Keep track of all business expenses and incomes.

- Regularly review your financials and adjust pricing, services, or expenses as needed to maximize profitability.

Legal Considerations:

- Ensure you have all necessary licenses and permits.

- Use contracts for all client work to protect both parties.

- Consider liability insurance to protect against potential claims.

Reinvest:

As you start making profits, consider reinvesting a portion back into the business for further growth, whether it's in marketing, hiring, training, or tools.

Remember, building a seven-figure business doesn't happen overnight. It requires persistence, adaptability, continuous learning, and the ability to face and overcome challenges. Surround yourself with a supportive network, and always keep the end goal in mind.

How I Scaled and Maintained an 8-Figure Online Company

Growing a seven-figure digital company to eight figures is a significant leap, requiring strategic expansion, diversification, and refinement of existing processes. Here's a roadmap of how I was able to achieve this:

Deepen Market Penetration:

- **Existing Client Expansion:** Offer more services or packages to current clients. Cross-sell and upsell.
- **Acquire Larger Clients:** Target higher-end clientele that can afford premium services.

Diversification:

- **New Services:** Introduce complementary services or products that align with current offerings.
- **New Markets:** Enter new geographic markets or verticals.

Operational Efficiency:

- **Automation:** Invest in tools to automate repetitive tasks, thus allowing the team to focus on strategy and growth.
- **Process Optimization:** Regularly review and refine operational processes to ensure optimal efficiency.
- **Outsourcing:** Consider outsourcing non-core activities, such as accounting or admin tasks, to focus on core competencies.

Talent Management:

- **Hire Strategically:** Bring in experienced individuals who can bring new expertise or manage larger teams.

- **Continuous Training:** Regularly upskill your team to stay ahead of industry trends and offer the best services.

- **Retention:** Ensure a positive work environment, competitive salaries, and growth opportunities to retain top talent.

Build Strategic Partnerships:

- Collaborate with complementary businesses to expand offerings or reach.

- Partner with industry influencers or thought leaders to boost credibility and reach.

Scale the Company Culture:

- Maintain a strong company culture even as the business grows.

- Communicate the company's vision and values regularly.

I hope this helps you if you are currently trying to start an online business or trying to grow your own online business to the 7-8 figure range. I created a FREE Mini Course on how I was able to generate $250,000 monthly from Facebook groups as a beginner called "FB Group Secrets."

Gain Access to the FREE Mini course Here:

https://officialpaulalex.com/FBgroupsecrets

Good luck on your digital marketing journey, and I'm looking forward to you becoming a Digital Millionaire!

CHAPTER 6

The Traits of Leadership and Business

Leading by example in business is how I was able to become an overnight success after six years of growing as a person but also being an entrepreneur. I didn't know everything. I didn't know everyone. And trust me when I say this, I was scared to start every single business because there's always the fear of the unknown. No matter at what stage of business you are at, you will have to always make changes, make important decisions, and adjust to different situations.

I wish I could give you a blueprint to show you exactly what to do in every single situation and how to lead your team into war. Every decision, action, and move that I made in business came from experience I already had. If it wasn't for me working in corporate America selling cleaning solutions to restaurant business owners, I would have never learned how to talk to the public and improve my career as a police officer.

If I couldn't properly communicate, then I wouldn't have been able to transition to a detective within two years of being in law enforcement. If I didn't have the experience of being a detective, leading dozens of police officers, investigators, and federal agents into very dangerous situations where one mistake can cause death or possibly put my team in danger, then I wouldn't know how to lead a sales team in a business that does quite well with an 80% closing ratio in sales.

At the end of the day, your experience will give you the traits of a leader. If you want your team to respect you and turn employees into leaders in your organization then make sure to follow the steps below:

Vision and Strategic Alignment:

Clear Vision:

Every successful business leader has a clear vision for the company's future. This vision serves as a guiding light, ensuring that all efforts are directed toward a common goal. Communicate this vision clearly and passionately to your team so they can understand their role in achieving it.

Strategic Thinking:

Beyond just having a vision, leaders need to develop and implement strategies to achieve it. This involves understanding the market dynamics, recognizing opportunities, and being proactive rather than merely reactive to challenges.

Empower and Invest in Your Team:

Delegation:

Recognize the strengths and weaknesses of your team members. Assign responsibilities based on their strengths, which not only ensures the task is done effectively but also boosts the morale and confidence of the individual.

Continuous Development:

Investing in the continuous learning and development of your employees pays off in the long run. This can be in the form of training, workshops, or even mentorship. When employees grow, the business grows.

Build a Culture of Accountability and Transparency:

Accountability:

Ensure that every member of the team, including yourself, is accountable for their actions. This fosters a culture of responsibility where everyone understands the implications of their decisions and actions on the broader business goals.

Open Communication:

Cultivate an environment where team members feel comfortable sharing their opinions, feedback, and concerns. This not only helps in early identification of potential problems but also fosters a sense of belonging and collaboration. Being transparent about the state of the business, whether it's good news or challenges ahead, can earn you the trust and respect of your team.

Remember, leadership in business isn't just about making profit-driven decisions; it's about inspiring, guiding, and nurturing the entire organization toward shared success.

CONCLUSION - CALL TO ACTION (CTA)

What's Next?

I personally wrote this book and put as much value as possible from my own experiences to help you understand everything I went through to reach the level I'm currently at.

I'm in the middle of moving to Miami, Florida.

I was born and raised in the San Francisco Bay Area and recently moved to San Diego in the past two years.

You may be wondering why I decided to move from California to Florida.

The answer is simple… GROWTH.

I'm growing more and more every single month as a person and business-minded individual.

Miami, Florida is currently the hub for digital marketing, and I'm looking forward to expanding all three of my companies.

Here are some stats for this year of 2023.

ATMTogether.com has generated over $20 million in revenue since the launch of the official program back in January 2021.

I believe we will be able to achieve over $25 million by the end of December 2023.

MerchantAutomation.com was launched this year in February of 2023, and we just hit our goal of over $2.8 million in revenue within eight months.

I believe MerchantAutomation.com will be able to reach the $5 million in revenue mark by the end of December 2023.

My newest venture, **Consulting Task Force**, which is my digital marketing company, just crossed the $100,000 mark in revenue since the launch of the program in January of 2023.

I estimate that Consulting Task Force will achieve a quarter of a million dollars by the end of December 2023.

I'm not telling you about my numbers to show off or to brag.

I'm telling you because I want to show you what the everyday person can achieve if you have the vision and determination to want more in life.

I'm a simple guy with a simple plan.

I just put in the work every single day.

With that being said, this all started with one simple question to myself: *What can I do today to move the needle in my life?*

You always have options in life.

Just pick one road and take it.

Imperfect ACTION.

I recommend reading this book 2-3 times and to think if I can do this and make this happen within a short amount of time (six years), then what is stopping you from executing on your vision.

Take care of yourself,
Paul

THANK YOU FOR READING MY JOURNEY!

Ready to start your journey?

I want to provide you with some additional value to help you on your entrepreneurship journey. Go to the website below to claim one of your FREE gifts from me.

www.officialpaulalex.com/Thankyou2023

I appreciate your interest in my book, and value your feedback as it helps me improve future versions. I would appreciate it if you could leave your honest, authentic review on Amazon.com with your feedback. Thank you!